Flavours of...

GLOUCESTERSHIRE
& THE COTSWOLDS

RECIPES

D1134278

Compiled by Julia Skinner

THE FRANCIS FRITH COLLECTION

www.francisfrith.com

First published in the United Kingdom in 2011 by The Francis Frith Collection®

This edition published exclusively for Identity Books in 2011 ISBN 978-1-84589-563-1

British Library Cataloguing in Publication Data

Flavours of Gloucestershire & the Cotswolds - Recipes
Compiled by Julia Skinner

The Francis Frith Collection
Unit 6, Oakley Business Park,
Wylye Road, Dinton,
Wiltshire SP3 5EU
Tel: +44 (0) 1722 716 376
Email: info@francisfrith.co.uk
www.francisfrith.com

Printed and bound in Malaysia

Front Cover: **GLOUCESTER, CHILDREN 1923** 73687xp
Frontispiece: **WOTTON-UNDER-EDGE, LONG STREET 1897** 39382

The colour-tinting is for illustrative purposes only, and is not intended to be historically accurate

CONTENTS

RECIPE

CHESTNUT SOUP

Chestnuts are said to have been introduced to Britain by the Romans. The Gloucestershire area is rich in Roman remains, and there is a saying 'scratch Gloucestershire and find Rome'. The city of Gloucester itself stands on the site of an old Roman fort which they called Glevum, and the Roman town of Cirencester ('Corinium') was one of the most important towns in Roman Britain. This makes an ideal soup for Christmas time. A tin of chestnut purée can also be used if preferred, instead of fresh chestnuts.

> 450g/1 lb chestnuts
> 1.2 litres/2 pints chicken or vegetable stock
> 4 tablespoonfuls cream
> 25g/1oz butter
> ¼ teaspoonful white pepper
> ½ teaspoonful salt
> ½ teaspoonful caster sugar
> A blade of mace

Cut the ends off the chestnuts, and roast them in a moderate oven (180°C/350°F/Gas Mark 4) for about 20 minutes, until the outer and inner skins will peel off easily. Remove all the skins and then put the chestnuts in a saucepan with the vegetable stock, white pepper, salt, pepper, mace and caster sugar. Simmer all together for 1 hour or longer, until the chestnuts are quite tender.

When the chestnuts are cooked, take out the blade of mace and discard. Rub the chestnuts through a fine sieve (or put through a blender), moistening them with a little of the stock. Rinse out the saucepan, and return the chestnut purée and stock to it. Add the cream, and bring the soup to just below boiling point, stirring well, then reduce heat, cover the pan and simmer gently for about 20 minutes, until it is quite smooth – it should have the consistency of thin cream, but add a little milk or stock if it is too thick. Check for seasoning, and adjust to taste if necessary.

CIRENCESTER, MARKET PLACE 1898 40965

RECIPE

WHITE FOAM SOUP

This is a light and tasty soup which is traditional to Gloucestershire. This recipe makes enough for about 6 people, so halve the quantities if you want to make less.

1 onion
1 stick of celery
1 clove of garlic
50g/2oz butter
25g/1oz plain flour
1.2 litres/2 pints of milk
A small piece of mace blade
2 eggs, separated
Salt and pepper
50g/2oz finely-grated cheese
1 tablespoonful of chopped fresh parsley

Chop the onion and celery very finely, and crush the garlic. Melt the butter in a large saucepan, stir in the flour and then gradually add the milk, stirring it thoroughly. Bring to the boil, stirring continually, then reduce the heat and simmer for 2 minutes. Add the onion, celery, garlic and blade of mace, and simmer the soup gently at a low heat until it is well flavoured.

Remove from heat and allow to cool slightly, then stir in the beaten yolks of the eggs. Reheat the soup but take care not to allow it to boil. Add salt and pepper to taste, and the grated cheese, still making sure that the soup does not boil.

Whisk or beat the egg whites to a stiff froth, and carefully fold half into the soup using a large metal spoon. Pour the rest of the egg white into a soup tureen or individual soup bowls, and pour the soup over. Sprinkle with the chopped fresh parsley, and serve with crispy fried croutons of bread.

RECIPE

SORREL SOUP

Common, or Garden, Sorrel is also known as Spinach Dock or Narrow-leaved Dock. It is a perennial herb that is often cultivated as a vegetable, but is also found growing wild. Sorrel has a pleasantly sharp flavour with a lemony tang and makes an excellent soup for the spring or summer. This traditional country recipe from Gloucestershire makes a large quantity, enough for about 8 people.

Sorrel should not be cooked in an aluminium or cast-iron pan, as the natural acids in the plant will react with the metal and affect the flavour.

> 450g/1 lb sorrel leaves
> 2.5 litres/4½ pints chicken stock
> 150ml/ ¼ pint cream
> 75g/3oz butter
> 2 egg yolks
> 1 large onion
> 2 tablespoonfuls of plain flour
> 2 tablespoonfuls of fresh breadcrumbs
> Salt and black pepper

Wash and chop the sorrel. Heat the butter in a saucepan and fry the chopped onion until it is transparent. Add the sorrel and cook for a few minutes to soften it. Sprinkle the flour over the vegetables and mix well, and cook for about 1 minute.

In another saucepan, bring the stock to the boil, then gradually add it to the vegetables, stirring all the time. Add the breadcrumbs, and season to taste. Bring to the boil, stirring continually, then reduce the heat, cover the pan and simmer gently for about 1 hour.

The soup can be liquidized at this stage if a smooth consistency is preferred, before continuing:

Beat the egg yolks with the cream and add a little of the hot soup to the mixture, stirring well, then gradually combine the mixture with the rest of the soup in the pan, stirring well, over heat, but not allowing the soup to boil. Serve with a swirl of extra cream and crispy fried croutons of bread.

RECIPE

SALMON WITH CUCUMBER SAUCE

The River Severn cuts right through Gloucestershire, and is famous for the salmon that are caught there; traditionally, they were caught by salmon fishermen using a special net on a Y-shaped frame known as a 'lave net'. Fishermen also used to trap salmon in funnel-shaped baskets placed across the river estuary, but these are rarely seen nowadays. Salmon or trout served with a cream and cucumber sauce is a traditional dish in many parts of England. This is an ideal dish for hot summer days.

> 1.8kg/4 lbs salmon, gutted and scaled
> A small amount of melted butter, for brushing on to the salmon
> 3 parsley or thyme sprigs
> Half a lemon, cut into 2 further segments
> 1 large cucumber, peeled
> 25g/1oz butter
> 115ml/4 fl oz dry white wine
> 3 tablespoonfuls of finely chopped dill
> 4 tablespoonfuls of sour cream, or natural yogurt if preferred
> Salt and pepper

Pre-heat the oven to 220°C/425°F/Gas Mark 7.

Season the salmon and brush it inside and out with melted butter. Place the herbs and lemon in the cavity. Wrap the salmon in foil, folding the edges together securely, then bake in the pre-heated oven for 15 minutes. Remove the fish from the oven and leave in the foil for 1 hour, then remove the skin from the salmon.

Meanwhile, halve the cucumber lengthways, scoop out the seeds, and dice the flesh. Place the cucumber in a colander, toss lightly with salt, leave for about 30 minutes to drain, then rinse well and pat dry.

Heat the butter in a small saucepan, add the cucumber and cook for about 2 minutes, until translucent but not soft. Add the wine to the pan and boil briskly until the cucumber is dry. Stir the dill and sour cream or yogurt into the cucumber. Season to taste and serve immediately with salmon.

RECIPE

SALMON BAKED IN PASTRY

900g/2 lbs fillet of salmon
Salt and pepper
Lemon juice
1 tablespoonful olive oil
675g/1½ lbs puff pastry
225g/8oz onions or shallots
Half a teaspoonful chopped tarragon
115g/4oz button mushrooms
1 egg, beaten, for glazing the pastry

Oven temperature: 190°C/375°F/Gas Mark 5.

Season the salmon with salt, pepper and lemon juice. Heat the olive oil in a large frying pan and lightly fry the salmon on both sides. Take the salmon out of the pan and leave to cool.

Roll out the puff pastry on a floured surface to form an oblong shape large enough to enclose the salmon. Chop the onions or shallots very finely, and sweat them in the pan the fish was cooked in, together with the tarragon. Allow to cool, then spread over one half of the pastry. Thinly slice the mushrooms and place them on top of the onions. Season with salt and pepper.

Place the salmon on top of the vegetables, fold over the other half of the pastry to enclose it all, and seal the edges. Place, folded side down, on a well-greased baking sheet and brush the top with beaten egg to glaze. Bake in the pre-heated oven for 1 hour, until the pastry is crisp and golden brown.

'A SURFEIT OF LAMPREYS ...'

Rather unattractive eel-like fish which are caught in the Severn are lampreys. These are parasitical, having jawless mouths with a ring of teeth that they use as a powerful sucker to latch on to other fish and feed on their blood, and also hitch a ride up the Severn estuary. They are sometimes called 'nine-eyes' locally, because they have seven gill slits running along their sides, which look like extra eyes.

Lampreys have two poisonous filaments running down their back which must be cut off before cooking. They are seldom eaten nowadays as their flesh is very rich and fatty, but in medieval times they were considered a great delicacy.

From the early Middle Ages it was customary for the Corporation of Gloucester to send a lamprey pie to the reigning monarch each Christmas; this tradition lasted up to 1836, although Gloucester still sends a Royal Lamprey Pie to the monarch to mark particularly special occasions – Queen Elizabeth II received one for her Coronation in 1953, and again for her Silver Jubilee in 1977.

King John (1167-1216) enjoyed lampreys so much that he once fined the city of Gloucester 40 marks for forgetting to send him his lamprey pie, obviously not put off by the fact that his great-grandfather, King Henry I, famously died in 1135 after gorging on a 'a surfeit of lampreys'.

GLOUCESTER, THE DOCKS 1950
G20052

'ELVERS'

On a dark night in February the River Severn is lit with hundreds of lights along both banks, each with a fisherman keenly waiting to catch elvers (baby eels) on the first spring tide of the season.... These are elvermen, who annually take their strange-looking nets to the river in the hope

GLOUCESTER FISHING FOR ELVERS 2004 G20701

of securing a large catch of the translucent, worm-like fish. These little elvers have taken three years to travel from the Sargasso Sea in the North Atlantic to the Severn at Gloucester, and if they are lucky enough to escape being caught, they will then remain here for a number of years before returning home again to breed. Elvers, for centuries a local delicacy, were once sold in pint mugs around the city streets of Gloucester before being cooked by housewives in a frying pan, together with the fat from a nice piece of bacon. Another local speciality was known as Elver Cakes, which was a form of pie. Sadly they are now far too expensive to be sold locally, for they command high prices around the world, but if you do manage to acquire some, here is a recipe for fried elvers:

> 450g/1 lb fresh elvers
> 15g/1oz seasoned flour
> Oil for deep frying
> 1 lemon

Wash the elvers well with salted water. Coat them with the seasoned flour, making sure that all parts are covered or they will stick together when they are fried. Heat the oil and deep-fry the elvers until they are crisp, then serve with lemon wedges.

RECIPE

BAKED STUFFED TROUT

Angling is a popular pastime in the Cotswolds, where there are a number of rivers and lakes where brown and rainbow trout, grayling, chubb, roach, pike and carp can be caught. One of the best Cotswold rivers is the Coln, which rises near Sevenhampton and flows through the Cotswolds before joining the Thames near Lechlade. There are also a number of commercial fisheries, many of which have been developed from former gravel pits, such as those at the Cotswolds Water Park near Cirencester.

> 4 trout, gutted and cleaned, with fins and gills removed
> 115g/4oz fresh breadcrumbs
> 115g/4oz butter
> Grated rind and juice of 1 lemon
> Salt and pepper to taste
> 1 egg yolk
> 25g/1oz plain flour
> 300ml/ ½ pint milk

Pre-heat the oven to 180°C/350°C/Gas Mark 4.

Melt half the butter in a heavy-bottomed pan, and add the breadcrumbs, lemon rind, salt and pepper. Remove from the heat and allow to cool a little, then beat in the egg yolk to form a firm stuffing. Use the stuffing to fill the cavity of each fish. Place the stuffed fish in a greased, ovenproof dish, dot the top with small knobs of butter, and bake in the pre-heated oven for 30 minutes.

Whilst the fish are cooking, melt the remaining butter in a saucepan, and stir in the flour to make a roux sauce. Cook gently for a few minutes, stirring occasionally, then gradually add the milk, stirring all time, and bring to the boil, still stirring continually, until the sauce has thickened. When the fish are cooked, pour the sauce into the dish with the fish and stir so that it combines with the fish juices. Add the lemon juice, then return the dish to the oven to cook for a further 5 minutes before serving.

RECIPE

GLOUCESTERSHIRE SQUAB PIE

The Cotswold Hills have always been famous for sheep rearing – indeed, the Old English word 'cots' in the name of the Cotswolds referred to a place where sheep were kept, and 'wolds' meant hills. Lamb features in many recipes from this region, such as Gloucestershire Squab Pie. Squab pies would probably have originally have been made with young pigeons, but over time it became more usual to make them with lamb and slices of cooking apple, flavoured with spices.

> 675g/1½ lbs lamb neck fillets, cut into 12 pieces
> 1 onion, thinly sliced
> 350g/12oz leeks, sliced
> 1 large cooking apple, peeled, cored and diced
> Half a teaspoonful of allspice
> Half a teaspoonful of freshly grated nutmeg
> 150ml/¼ pint lamb, beef or vegetable stock
> 225g/8oz shortcrust pastry
> Beaten egg or milk to glaze
> Salt and pepper

Pre-heat the oven to 200°C/400°F/Gas Mark 6.

Layer the meat, onion, leek and apple in a pie dish, sprinkling in the spices and seasoning as you go, to taste. Pour in the stock.

Roll out the pastry to 2cm (¾ inch) larger than the top of the pie dish. Cut a narrow strip from around the pastry, fit it around the dampened rim of the dish, then brush with water. Lay the pastry over the dish, and press the edges together to seal them. Brush the pastry lid with beaten egg or milk, and make a hole in the centre.

Bake the pie in the pre-heated oven for 20 minutes, then reduce the oven temperature to 180°C/350°F/Gas Mark 4 and continue to cook for 1-1¼ hours, covering the pie with foil if the pastry starts to brown too much.

CHIPPING NORTON, A VIEW OF THE COTSWOLDS c1960 C288067

The Cotswolds are an upland area of limestone. The escarpment, 'the Cotswold edge', rises above the broad valley of the River Severn, and the land slopes gently away eastward. The main area of the Cotswolds is contained in Gloucestershire, but it extends eastwards into Oxfordshire and to some degree into Worcestershire, Warwickshire, Wiltshire and Somerset. The Cotswold region has been designated as an Area of Outstanding Natural Beauty.

RECIPE

LAMB CHOPS PORTMANTEAU'D

This dish was named after a small travelling bag known as a 'portmanteau' which the lamb chops resemble when they have been stuffed with their filling and cooked. The Cotswolds were prime fox-hunting territory, and this used to be a popular dish to serve to gentlemen at hunt breakfasts, to sustain them for a day spent in the saddle following the hounds. Thick lamb chops need to be chosen to make this.

> 4 thick loin lamb chops, trimmed of fat
> 50g/2oz butter
> 8 chicken livers, trimmed and chopped into small pieces
> 8 mushrooms, finely chopped
> 1 egg, beaten
> 50g/2oz dried breadcrumbs, seasoned with salt and pepper

Pre-heat the oven to 200°C/400°F/Gas Mark 6.

Use a very sharp knife to cut a horizontal slit right up to the bone in each chop, to make a pocket large enough to be stuffed.

Melt half the butter in a frying pan, add the chicken livers and mushrooms and fry gently for 4-5 minutes, until soft but not browned. Leave to cool for a few minutes, then use the mixture to stuff the pockets in the lamb chops. Sew up the pockets with trussing thread.

Dip each chop first in the beaten egg and then into the seasoned breadcrumbs, pressing the breadcrumbs on with your fingers, to make sure that the chops are coated thoroughly. Place the chops in a baking dish. Melt the remaining butter and pour it over the chops. Bake in the pre-heated oven for 7-10 minutes, depending on how 'pink' you like your lamb, then turn the chops over and bake for a further 7-10 minutes, until the chops are golden brown on both sides. Serve at once, whilst the chops are piping hot and crispy.

STOW-ON-THE-WOLD, THE SQUARE
c1950 S260024

'Stow-on-the-Wold, where the wind blows cold' warns an old local adage about this Cotswold town perched 800 feet above sea level on a rounded tump. The surrounding countryside is excellent sheep country, and in past centuries the local wool merchants thrived and built themselves fine houses in Stow. The heart of the town is its Square, where stalls were first set up for the Thursday market (which continues to this day) in 1107. Local lore says the reason the buildings were clustered so tightly around the Square at Stow-on-the-Wold was to keep the wind off the farmers on market days. Daniel Defoe visited the town in the early 18th century and recorded that 20,000 sheep were sold at Stow's market in the year prior to his visit. Squeezed between the buildings in Stow's Square are alleys, known locally as 'tures' (an abbreviation of 'aperture'). These follow the patterns of old burgage strips, and on market days in time gone by, sheep were driven in single file along these narrow ways to be counted.

RECIPE

PORK WITH APPLES AND CIDER SAUCE

Think of Gloucestershire and cider, and Laurie Lee's famous book 'Cider With Rosie' comes to mind. The book chronicles the author's childhood in the picturesque hillside village of Slad, near Stroud, and charts the changes in this rural settlement during the 1920s. Slad, set in its wooded valley, is still much as it was during Laurie Lee's boyhood. The title of 'Cider with Rosie' refers to the young Laurie being seduced by Rosie Burdock underneath a hay wagon after drinking cider from a flagon for the first time: *'Never to be forgotten, that first long secret drink of golden fire, juice of those valleys and of that time, wine of wild orchards, of russet summer, of plump red apples …'.* Use Gloucestershire cider to make a delicious creamy sauce to accompany pork in this recipe.

> 25g/1oz butter
> 500g/1¼ lbs pork fillet or tenderloin, cut into small pieces
> 12 baby onions or shallots, peeled and left whole
> 2 teaspoonfuls grated lemon rind
> 300ml/ ½ pint dry Gloucestershire cider
> 150ml/ ¼ pint stock
> 2 crisp eating apples, cored and sliced but not peeled
> 3 tablespoonfuls chopped fresh parsley
> 100ml/3½ fl oz whipping cream
> Salt and pepper

Heat the butter in a large sauté or frying pan, and brown the pork in batches. Transfer the pork to a bowl. Add the onions to the pan and cook gently until they are soft. Stir in the lemon rind, cider and stock, increase heat and boil for a few minutes. Return the pork to the pan, reduce heat and cook gently for 25-30 minutes, until the meat is tender. Add the apples to the pan and cook for a further 5 minutes.

Use a slotted spoon to transfer the pork, apples and onions to a warmed serving dish, and keep warm. Stir the cream and parsley into the cooking pan, and allow the sauce to bubble so that it thickens slightly. Season to taste, then pour over the pork and serve whilst it is hot.

GLOUCESTERSHIRE OLD SPOTS PIGS

The Gloucestershire Old Spots breed of pig, characterised by large black spots on its skin, was developed to thrive on the whey that was a by-product of Gloucestershire's cheese industry, and, particularly, windfall apples in the county's orchards – it is often referred to as 'The Orchard Pig'. The meat is well-flavoured and makes excellent Gloucester (or Gloster) Sausages, but above all this is the pork to seek out at good butchers and farmers' markets if you want to serve up a great joint of roast pork with wonderful crispy, puffy crackling. Do not be put off by a good layer of fat on the joint, as this is where much of the flavour is. To ensure really good crackling, pat the skin of the joint dry with kitchen paper before cooking, then score the skin of the joint with a very sharp knife (a Stanley knife is ideal), making a number of deep, parallel cuts at regular intervals. Then rub all over the skin with plenty of salt, making sure that you also rub it well into the slash lines (a mixture of sea salt and regular kitchen salt is best), put the joint into a shallow roasting dish, and do not add any oil or fat – plastering extra fat on the joint is the death of good crackling!

A boned loin joint of around 1.5kg (about 3½ lbs) of good quality pork with a good layer of fatty skin will give you a succulent roast with excellent crackling, and is a handy size for four or five people. Prepare the joint as above, then put it into a pre-heated oven at 245°C/475°F/Gas Mark 9. Roast for 25 minutes, then reduce the heat to 190°C/375°F/Gas Mark 5 and roast for a further one hour. You won't need to baste the joint during cooking as the fat in the meat will keep it moist. If the crackling is not quite hard and crisp at the end of the cooking time, turn up the heat to 220°C/425°F/Gas Mark 7 and cook for a further 10-15 minutes. Remove the meat from the oven, cover with foil and allow to 'rest' for 15-20 minutes before carving the pork into slices, and serve with strips of crackling, apple sauce, vegetables, gravy and roast, boiled or mashed potatoes.

STROUD, KING STREET 1910
62677

RECIPE

GAMMON AND APRICOTS

Gloucestershire bacon and ham was the subject of much praise in 'The Magazine of Domestic Economy' in 1838, which reported that 'In Gloucestershire, especially in the Forest of Dean, the swine feed heavily on beech mast, acorns, and the various productions of the woodlands. This imparts great sweetness and solidity to their flesh'. This traditional dish from the Cotswolds was often served at harvest time, when apricots were ripe. Canned apricots can also be used if preferred, well drained and chopped.

> 450g/1 lb gammon rashers, or thin gammon steaks
> 25g/1oz butter
> 350g/12oz fresh apricots
> 25g/1oz sultanas
> Pepper
> 300ml/ ½ pint stock
> 675g/1½ lbs potatoes

Pre-heat the oven to 180°C/350°F/Gas Mark 4.

Melt the butter in a frying pan and fry the gammon rashers or steaks lightly on both sides, then put the gammon into a casserole dish.

Wash and dry the apricots, then cut each apricot in half with a sharp knife, following the indentation, and remove its stone. Coarsely chop the apricot halves, then put the chopped apricots and sultanas on top of the gammon, and season to taste with pepper. Pour over the stock. Peel the potatoes, cut them into thin slices and arrange them on top of the gammon and apricots.

Cover the casserole dish with its lid, and bake in the pre-heated oven for 1 hour, or until the potato slices are tender.

Flavours of...
GLOUCESTERSHIRE & THE COTSWOLDS
MEAT, POULTRY AND GAME

COLEFORD, THE TOWN HALL
c1950 C315027

CIRENCESTER, OXEN TEAM IN CIRENCESTER PARK 1898 40986

RECIPE

STUFFED SKIRT OF BEEF

This is a very old Gloucestershire recipe for an economical and nourishing way of cooking one of the cheaper cuts of beef.

1kg/2 lbs skirt of beef
50g/2oz dripping (or oil, for browning the meat)
225g/8oz onion, finely chopped
1.2 litres/2 pints beef stock
Salt and pepper
115g/4oz carrots, sliced
115g/4oz turnip, peeled and chopped into small chunks
50g/2oz cornflour
2 tablespoonfuls of water

For the stuffing:
115g/4oz medium oatmeal
50g/2oz shredded suet
1 tablespoonful of chopped fresh parsley and other herbs of choice
25g/1oz onion, very finely chopped
A little milk

Buy the skirt of beef in one piece. Remove the skin and slice a deep pocket in the meat with a sharp knife. Combine all the stuffing ingredients together, using just enough milk to bind it to a stiff consistency. Fill the pocket in the meat with the stuffing and sew up the opening with trussing thread. Melt the dripping (or oil) in a large, heavy saucepan and brown the meat and the onions. Add the stock, and season to taste, if necessary. Bring to the boil, then reduce heat, cover the pan and simmer very gently for 2½ - 3 hours, until the meat is tender. About 45 minutes before the end of the cooking time, add the carrots and turnip to the pan. When the meat is ready to serve, blend the cornflour with the water, and add it to the pan to thicken the gravy. Lift out the meat and remove the trussing thread, and serve it on a hot dish surrounded by the carrots and turnips, and serve the gravy separately.

RECIPE

GLOUCESTERSHIRE COTTAGE PIE

This is traditionally served cold, with salad, and is a good way of using leftover beef and gravy.

> 450g/1 lb cooked beef
> 115g/4oz cooked bacon or ham
> 225g/8oz cold potatoes
> 115g/4oz fresh breadcrumbs
> 25g/1oz butter or margarine
> 1 egg
> 2 onions, peeled and chopped
> Salt and pepper
> Leftover gravy

Pre-heat the oven to 180°C/350°F/Gas Mark 4.

Mince the cold beef and bacon together, and season well. Fry the chopped onions in the butter or margarine until soft and starting to brown, then add enough gravy to cover and boil for 10 minutes.

Mix together the egg, meat, bacon, potatoes and breadcrumbs, then add this to the gravy mixture and combine it all well together.

Turn the mixture into a greased pie dish, or a loaf tin lined with foil, and bake for 30 minutes in the pre-heated oven.

'ROOK PIE, ANYONE?'

Rook Pie was often eaten by country people in the past, sometimes served with the feet of the rooks sticking out of the centre of the crust, although a more usual way was to take just the breast and upper legs of the bird for the pie. Only the younger birds were used, so Rook Pie was usually eaten in spring and early summer. Other traditional dishes which were eaten in this area in former centuries, and which are very much not to modern tastes, were Lambs' Tail Pie, made from the docked tails of lambs in the spring, and Muggety Pie, with a jelly-like filling made from the umbilical cords of new-born calves.

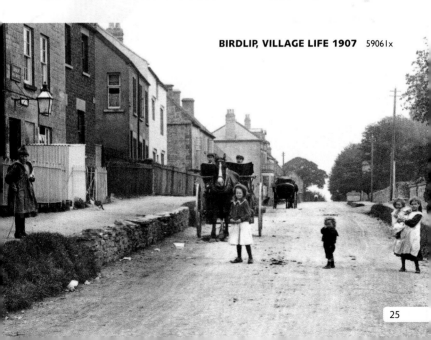

BIRDLIP, VILLAGE LIFE 1907   59061x

25

TEWKESBURY, HIGH STREET 1891 29384

RECIPE

SIRLOIN STEAKS WITH TEWKESBURY MUSTARD

In past centuries, the town of Tewkesbury gave its name to a method of making a particularly thick, fiery mustard which included horseradish in its ingredients. It was originally made, transported and sold in the form of small balls of mustard mixture which had been dried to aid preservation. The mustard balls would be broken apart when they were needed for use and then mixed to a creamy consistency with liquid (which could be water, wine, ale or cider). The mustard was mentioned by Shakespeare in 'Henry IV, Part 2', when Sir John Falstaff says 'His wit's as thick as Tewkesbury mustard'. The mustard also gave rise to a phrase used in Gloucestershire to describe someone whose expression is sad, severe or stern: 'He looks as if he lived on Tewkesbury mustard'. The making of Tewkesbury mustard was revived in the late 20th century. Several manufacturers now produce it commercially, and the Waitrose supermarket chain sells its own-label version. Because Tewkesbury mustard is made with finely-grated horseradish as well as mustard seeds, it goes particularly well with beef. This recipe is for four people – increase the quantities for more.

> 4 sirloin steaks
> 50g/2oz Tewkesbury mustard
> 15g/ ½ oz plain flour
> 2 tablespoonfuls chopped fresh parsley
> 2 tablespoonfuls chopped fresh thyme

Pre-heat the grill. Mix together the mustard and the flour, and spread the mixture on top of the sirloin steaks. Line the grill pan with tin foil and sprinkle the foil with the chopped fresh herbs. Place the steaks on the foil, on top of the herbs, and grill for 5-15 minutes (depending on how you like your steak cooked), turning the steaks frequently until they are cooked to taste.

RECIPE

GLOUCESTERSHIRE CHEESE AND ALE

Gloucestershire is famous for its Double Gloucester cheese, with its characteristic light orange colour that is achieved by the addition of annatto, a natural colouring. In former times, the milk of different breeds of cow was used to make different cheeses, and traditionally the Old Gloucester breed was considered the only cow for making Double Gloucester cheese – the milk from this breed had very small fat globules, which gave the cheese a special fine texture. Gloucester cheese used to be made in two varieties, Single Gloucester and Double Gloucester, but only Double Gloucester is made nowadays. Traditionally, Double Gloucester was produced on farms using mainly the morning's milk, with just a little from the evening's milking, and was made in large cheeses weighing between 15 and 25 pounds that took several months to mature. Single Gloucester was made from either the morning's milk or skimmed evening milk and much smaller cheeses were made, weighing between nine and twelve pounds – this did not need ripening, and was mainly eaten on the farms where it was made, rather than sold. Double Gloucester melts well so is an ideal cheese for toasting and cooking with, and this recipe is the Gloucestershire version of toasted cheese. This makes enough to 4-8 people, depending on appetite!

> 225g/8oz Double Gloucester cheese
> 1 teaspoonful of English mustard
> 300ml/ ½ pint brown ale
> 8 thick slices of wholemeal bread

Pre-heat the oven to 230°C/450°F/Gas Mark 8. Grate the cheese and place it in an ovenproof dish. Spread the surface of the cheese with mustard, and pour on the ale. Bake in the pre-heated oven until the cheese had melted –about 5-10 minutes. Whilst the cheese is melting, toast the bread slices. Place the pieces of toast in individual wide serving bowls, and when the cheese and ale mixture is ready, pour some over each piece of toast and serve immediately, whilst it is piping hot.

RECIPE

GLOUCESTER CHEESE STEW

This tasty cheese and potato bake makes an ideal supper dish.

> 450g/1 lb potatoes
> 275ml/ ½ pint milk
> Salt and freshly ground black pepper
> 3 onions
> 225g/8oz Double Gloucester cheese, grated

Peel the potatoes, cut them into thin slices and place in a saucepan with the milk. Season with salt and pepper, then simmer them gently until almost tender (10-15 minutes).

Pre-heat the oven to 180°C/350°F/Gas Mark 4.

Take the potato slices out of the pan, and reserve the milk. Peel the onions and chop them finely. Grease a medium-sized casserole or ovenproof dish. Put layers of potato, onion and cheese into the dish, seasoning each layer, finishing with a layer of cheese. Pour over the milk that the potatoes were cooked in.

Bake the dish, uncovered, for one hour in the pre-heated oven, until the topping is crisp and golden brown.

J. BROWN
WATCH MAKER.

WOTTON-UNDER-EDGE, CHILDREN IN LONG STREET 1897 39384x

RECIPE

COTSWOLD CHEESE DUMPLINGS

These traditional savoury dumplings can be served hot with vegetables or a tomato sauce, or cold with a salad or as snacks with drinks. They can be made with any hard cheese of choice, but in this recipe the cheese marketed as Cotswold Cheese is used – a Double Gloucester Cheese with the addition of chives and onions.

> 50g/2oz Cotswold Cheese
> 25g/1oz butter or margarine
> 1 egg, beaten
> Salt and pepper
> 50g/2oz fresh breadcrumbs
> 25g/1oz dried breadcrumbs
> Fat or oil for frying

Grate the cheese finely. Beat the butter or margarine until it is creamy. Mix the grated cheese and creamed fat together, then add the beaten egg, and salt and pepper to taste. Combine the mixture with enough of the fresh breadcrumbs to form a stiff dough.

Turn the dough out onto a lightly floured board, and form it into small balls, or dumplings. Roll the dumplings in the dried breadcrumbs to coat them, then fry in hot fat until golden brown.

RECIPE

GLOUCESTERSHIRE POTATO CAKES

This traditional recipe makes a tasty supper dish.

> 450g/1 lb potatoes
> 25g/1oz butter or margarine
> 115g/4oz plain flour
> 115g/4oz Double Gloucester cheese, grated
> 2 eggs, beaten
> Salt and pepper
> Fat or oil for frying

Cook the potatoes in boiling salted water for 15-10 minutes until they are tender. Drain the potatoes then mash them with the butter or margarine. Add the flour and cheese and mix everything together thoroughly. Add the beaten eggs, season to taste with salt and pepper, and combine the mixture well.

Flour your hands and form the mixture into about 8 small cakes, and flatten them slightly. Heat the fat or oil in a frying pan and fry the potato cakes for a few minutes on both sides until they are golden brown.

RECIPE

SAVOURY CARROT PUDDING

This recipe for a savoury steamed pudding comes from Dursley, which was once a wool and cloth manufacturing town of some importance. Dursley's quaint yellow Market House was erected in 1738 and stands on 12 arches. The upper storey was used as a town hall, whilst market business was conducted on the open arcade of the ground floor – at one time, the local cheese and butter market was held there. Local people were so grateful to Queen Anne for money given to repair the parish church tower after part of it fell down in 1699 that they placed a statue of her in the upper niche of the Market House.

> 225g/8oz grated carrots
> 450g/1 lb cooked and sieved potatoes
> 225g/8oz sausage meat
> Salt and pepper
> A pinch of grated nutmeg
> 1 teaspoonful chopped fresh parsley
> 1 onion, finely chopped
> 1 egg, beaten
> A little milk or stock, for missing

Mix together the carrots, potatoes and sausage meat with the seasoning and beaten egg, adding a little milk or stock if necessary if the mixture seems to dry. Place the mixture in a greased pudding basin, and cover with pleated greaseproof paper (to allow room for rising during cooking) and foil, and tie down firmly.

Place the pudding basin in a large saucepan of boiling water and cover the pan with its lid. Steam for about 2 hours, topping up the pan with more boiling water when necessary, and ensuring that the pan does not boil dry. Serve with brown gravy.

DURSLEY, MARKET HOUSE c1947   D72028

BROADWAY, HIGH STREET c1955   B222048

Just inside Worcestershire is the Cotswold village of Broadway, sometimes described as the prettiest village in England, with its handsome houses in honey-hued stone and a village green shaded by chestnut trees. Now the major tourist centre of the north Cotswolds, back in the 17th century Broadway was a thriving staging post, and horse-drawn carriages by the dozen stopped to feed and water en route to London from Worcester. At that time, over 30 inns in the village offered passengers refreshment and accommodation. This lucrative trade came to an end with the arrival of the railway, and the end of stagecoaches, but the railways enabled the surrounding countryside to be developed into one of the country's most important market gardening areas, sited as it is on the edge of the fertile Vale of Evesham.

RECIPE

PLUM AND WALNUT CRUMBLE

From the great resources of the nearby Evesham Vale and Severn Valley, fruit has always been easily available in the area, particularly apples, damsons and plums. Gloucestershire was also noted in the past for walnuts, especially around Arlingham, near Stroud. In 1807 Thomas Rudge commented on the walnut trees there in his 'General View of the Agriculture of Gloucestershire': 'In the parish of Arlingham there are more, perhaps, than in many other parishes combined; so abundant, indeed, is the fruit this year (1805) that it is become an article of commerce, and two vessels are now being laded with walnuts for Scotland … the produce of a tree is highly valuable, as 20,000 are not considered an extravagant calculation for a large tree.' This recipe celebrates the place of both plums and walnuts in the region's culinary heritage.

> 75g/3oz walnut pieces
> 75g/3oz butter or margarine, diced
> 175g/6oz plain flour
> 175g/6oz demerara sugar
> 1kg/2 lbs plums, halved and stoned

Pre-heat the oven to 180°C/350°F/Gas Mark 4.

Spread the nuts on a baking sheet and place in the oven for 8-10 minutes, until they are evenly coloured.

Butter a 1.2 litre (2 pint) baking dish. Put the plums into the dish and stir in the nuts and half the demerara sugar. Rub the butter or margarine into the flour until the mixture resembles coarse crumbs. Stir in the remaining sugar and continue to rub in until fine crumbs are formed. Cover the fruit with the crumb mixture and press it down lightly. Bake the pudding in the pre-heated oven for about 45 minutes, until the top is golden brown and the fruit tender. Serve with custard or cream.

RECIPE

CRUNDLE PUDDING

This recipe comes from the village of Weston Subedge, near Chipping Campden.

> 50g/2oz plain flour
> 50g/2oz butter
> 50g/2oz caster sugar
> 1 egg, separated
> 300ml/ ½ pint milk

Pre-heat the oven to 180°C/350°C/Gas Mark 4.

Grease an ovenproof pie dish. Cream the butter and sugar together until light and fluffy, then mix in the flour. Beat the white of the egg until it is stiff then add the egg yolk to it and beat again. Add the egg to the mixture.

Just before putting the pudding in the oven, add the milk, stirring it in gradually – this must only be done at the very last moment. Turn out the mixture into the prepared pie dish and bake in the pre-heated oven for about 30 minutes.

This was traditionally served with warmed black treacle and cream.

RECIPE

CHELTENHAM PUDDING

175g/6oz plain flour
1 teaspoonful baking powder
Half a teaspoonful grated nutmeg
A pinch of salt
175g/6oz shredded suet
75g/3oz sugar
75g/3oz fresh breadcrumbs
50g/2oz raisins
50g/2oz currants
Grated rind of half a lemon
2 eggs, beaten
150ml/ ¼ pint milk

Pre-heat the oven to 190°C/375°F/Gas Mark 5.

Sift the flour, baking powder, nutmeg and salt together into a mixing bowl. Mix in the suet, sugar, breadcrumbs, dried fruit and lemon rind. Stir in the beaten eggs and milk. Beat the mixture well to make a stiff, smooth batter.

Pour the batter into a greased ovenproof dish and bake in the pre-heated oven for 1½ hours.

When cooked, turn out and serve with either a sweet sauce, custard or cream.

POST OFFICE

CHELTENHAM, THE PROMENADE 1923   73481

BISLEY, THE SEVEN SPRINGS 1910 62696

HEG PEG DUMP

St Margaret, the patron saint of safe childbirth, was a popular saint in the Middle Ages. Her feast day on 20th July was particularly remembered in Gloucestershire, when a special pudding known as Heg Peg Dump was made. This was traditionally a suetcrust dumpling containing wild fruit gathered from the hedges, such as plums or damsons, hence the strange name: Heg for hedgerow, Peg for Margaret (Peg or Peggy is a pet form of Margaret), and Dump for dumpling.

<u>For the suetcrust pastry:</u>
225g/8oz self-raising flour
Half a teaspoonful salt
1 teaspoonful baking powder
115g/4oz shredded suet
150ml/ ¼ pint cold water

<u>For the filling:</u>
450g/1 lb plums or damsons, stoned
225g/8oz cooking apples, peeled, cored and cut into slices
175g/6oz sugar
1 tablespoonful water

Sift the flour, salt and baking powder into a bowl. Add the suet and mix together lightly, adding enough water to mix to a soft dough. Turn out the dough onto a lightly floured surface and knead the dough until it is smooth and pliable. Save a third of the dough to make a lid and roll out the rest thinly. Use the rolled out pastry to line a greased 1.2 litre (2 pint) pudding basin. Fill the pastry-lined pudding basin with alternate layers of the fruit and sugar. Pour in the tablespoonful of water. Moisten the edges of the pudding pastry with water, and cover with a lid rolled out from the reserved pastry. Press the edges firmly together to seal them. Cover the pudding basin with a lid made of pleated greaseproof paper and then another of foil, and tie down securely with string. Place the pudding basin in a large pan of boiling water, cover the pan with its lid and steam for 2½ - 3 hours, replenishing the pan with more boiling water when necessary, and ensuring that the pan does not boil dry. When the pudding is cooked, serve it from the basin with custard or cream.

RECIPE

OLDBURY TARTS

These small gooseberry tarts (more accurately pies) are named after Oldbury-on-Severn, a village south of Berkeley, where they were often made for Whitsuntide. When you make them, make sure that the edges are well sealed or the sugar will leak out and burn. Oldbury Tarts should be eaten by hand, and are full of juice which runs out when they are bitten into. There is a tradition that there should be 21 points in the crimping that forms a decorative edge around the top of each tart.

> 450g/1 lb plain flour
> 115g/4oz lard
> 115g/4oz butter
> 140ml/5 fl oz boiling water
> 700g/1½ lbs gooseberries, washed, topped and tailed
> 4 dessertspoonfuls demerara sugar
> 1 egg, beaten, to glaze

Sieve the flour into a bowl and make a well in the centre. Cut the lard and the butter into pieces and put into the well in the flour. Pour the boiling water over the fat and stir until it melts, mixing in the flour to make a soft paste. Thinly roll out two-thirds of the pastry on a lightly-floured surface and cut it into 15 cm (6 inch) rounds. Hand-raise the edges of each pastry round by pleating the sides 4 or 5 times and bringing them up to form a pie shell. Put the prepared gooseberries together with one dessertspoon of brown sugar into the centre of each shell. From the remaining third of pastry, cut an equal number of smaller circles. Cover each pie shell with a lid made from one of the smaller rounds, moisten the edges, and pinch them together very well all round the tart, to seal the edges and form a decorative rim. Use a sharp knife to cut a small hole in the top of each lid to allow steam to escape during cooking. Transfer the tarts to greased baking sheets and chill in the fridge for 2-3 hours to allow the pastry to firm up.

When ready to cook, pre-heat the oven to 230°C/450°F/Gas Mark 8. Brush each tart with a little beaten egg to glaze, then bake in the pre-heated oven for 10 minutes, then reduce the oven temperature to 180°C/350°F/Gas Mark 4 and bake for a further 20 minutes.

BERKELEY, A SHOP 1904 51752v

RECIPE

BLAKENEY FRITTERS

This recipe comes from the village of Blakeney, on the eastern edge of the Forest of Dean. Although these are called fritters, they are actually more like biscuits. This amount should make about 10 fritters.

> 75g/3oz plain flour
> 50g/2oz butter or margarine
> 25g/1oz caster sugar
> 1 egg, separated
> Jam of choice

Pre-heat the oven to 180°C/350°F/Gas Mark 4. Lightly grease a baking sheet.

Put the flour in a bowl and rub in the butter or margarine. Add the sugar and egg yolk, and work the mixture to a paste. Roll little balls of the mixture in your hands and put them on to the greased baking sheet, spacing them well apart. Use the end of a wooden spoon handle to make a hole in each ball, but not quite all through to the other side, and brush them over with a little egg white.

Bake just above the centre of the pre-heated oven for about 30 minutes, until they are just turning golden brown. Remove from the oven and slide the balls onto a wire rack to cool. When cool, fill the hole in each biscuit with a jam of your choice. Store in an airtight container.

RECIPE

GLOUCESTER TARTS

This amount should make about 16 tarts.

> 175g/6oz shortcrust pastry
> 50g/2oz butter or margarine
> 50g/2oz caster sugar
> 1 egg
> 1 teaspoonful almond essence
> 50g/2oz ground rice
> Raspberry or apricot jam
> A little icing sugar, to finish

Pre-heat the oven to 180°C/350°F/Gas Mark 4.

Grease and lightly flour 16 patty tins. Roll out the pastry on a lightly-floured surface and cut it into rounds about 5cm (2 inch) in diameter, and use the rounds to line the patty tins.

Cream the sugar and butter or margarine together until it is light and fluffy. Beat the egg and carefully add it to the creamed mixture, a little at a time, and then stir in the almond essence. Use a large metal spoon to fold in the ground rice and combine the mixture thoroughly together.

Put a spoonful of jam into the bottom of each pastry-lined patty tin, and then cover with a good spoonful of the ground rice mixture. Bake the tarts in the pre-heated oven for about 15-20 minutes, until the filling is lightly golden and firm to the touch. Leave to cool on a wire rack before eating. Sift a dusting of icing sugar over them before serving.

GLOUCESTER, SOUTHGATE STREET
1900 45508

RECIPE

APPLE COBS

Apple Cobs is the Gloucestershire name for Apple Dumplings, which can be made with either shortcrust or suetcrust pastry.

> 4 large cooking apples
> 50g/2oz soft brown sugar
> 25g/1oz butter
> Half a teaspoonful cinnamon
> Grated rind of 1 lemon
> 225g/8oz shortcrust or suetcrust pastry
> Milk to glaze
> Caster sugar

Pre-heat the oven to 180°C/350°F/Gas Mark 4.

Peel and core the apples.

Divide the pastry into four equal pieces. Roll each piece out into a square big enough to wrap around an apple. Place one apple in the centre of each square. Mix the sugar, lemon peel and cinnamon together and use the mixture to fill the cavity of each apple, and place a knob of butter on top of the mixture.

Dampen the edges of each piece of pastry with water, and fold up the corners to meet at the top like a parcel, and enclose each apple. Pinch the pastry edges well together to seal.

Place the dumplings – join downwards – in a greased ovenproof dish and brush with milk to glaze. Bake in the pre-heated oven for about half an hour – test by sticking a skewer into the dumpling to make sure the apple is soft. Sprinkle with caster sugar, and serve with custard or cream.

RECIPE

SHERRY CAKE

This rich and boozy fruit cake is another recipe that developed from the fox-hunting heritage of the Cotswolds. It was often served to riders returning home after a long day out in the hunting field.

115g/4oz butter or margarine
115g/4oz caster sugar
3 eggs, separated
225g/8oz plain flour
A pinch of salt
115g/4oz ground almonds
115g/4oz currants
50g/2oz candied mixed peel
50g/2oz glacé cherries, cut into halves
50g/2oz chopped almonds
2 glasses sherry
1 teaspoonful bicarbonate of soda
2 teaspoonfuls vinegar

Pre-heat the oven to 220°C/425°F/Gas Mark 7.

Grease and line a 20cm (8 inch) cake tin. Beat together the butter and sugar until light and fluffy. Add the egg yolks one at a time, beating the mixture well between each addition. Sift the flour and salt into the mixture and gradually stir it in to mix. Stir in the ground almonds, currants, mixed peel, cherries and chopped almonds. Add 1 glass of sherry, and beat the mixture well. Whisk the egg whites until they are stiff and stand in peaks, then fold into the cake mixture, using a large metal spoon. Dissolve the bicarbonate of soda in the vinegar and add to the cake mixture, then beat well. Turn the cake mixture into the prepared cake tin and cover the top with a double layer of greaseproof paper. Bake in the pre-heated oven for 10 minutes, then reduce the oven temperature to 160°C/325°F/Gas Mark 3 and bake for a further 2 hours. When the cake is cooked, remove from the oven and carefully pour the other glass of sherry over the cake whilst it is still hot – the sherry will soak into the cake. Leave the cake in the tin to cool before turning out. This cake will keep well, stored in an airtight tin.

RECIPE

GINGERBREAD HUSBANDS

The biscuits usually known as Gingerbread Men are called Gingerbread Husbands in Gloucestershire. In former times it was the custom in many parts of rural Gloucestershire on Twelfth Night (the evening of January 5th, 12 nights after Christmas) to light thirteen fires in honour of Jesus and his twelve apostles, and then immediately stamp out the fire representing Judas, the apostle who betrayed Jesus. Seed cake (flavoured with caraway seeds), plum cake and gingerbread husbands would then be eaten as people stood around the warmth of the remaining twelve fires, and cider would be drunk as the forthcoming harvest was toasted.

> 225g/8oz plain flour
> Half a teaspoonful bicarbonate of soda
> 1 teaspoonful ground ginger
> 275g/10oz golden syrup
> 75g/3oz lard or margarine

Pre-heat the oven to 180°C/350°F/Gas Mark 4.

Sift the flour, bicarbonate of soda and ginger into a mixing bowl. Gently heat the golden syrup and lard or margarine in a saucepan until they have melted, then stir into the flour and mix together well to form a dough. Knead the dough lightly, then turn it out on to a lightly floured surface and roll it out thinly. Cut the dough into gingerbread man shapes using a shaped cutter. Place the gingerbread husbands on to greased baking trays and bake in the pre-heated oven for about 10 minutes, until they are golden brown but not burnt. Leave on a wire rack to cool before decorating the biscuits with faces, buttons etc with coloured icing – in Gloucestershire they were often gilded.

CHALFORD, THE VILLAGE 1910 62713

FRANCIS FRITH

PIONEER VICTORIAN PHOTOGRAPHER

Francis Frith, founder of the world-famous photographic archive, was a complex and multi-talented man. A devout Quaker and a highly successful Victorian businessman, he was philosophical by nature and pioneering in outlook. By 1855 he had already established a wholesale grocery business in Liverpool, and sold it for the astonishing sum of £200,000, which is the equivalent today of over £15,000,000. Now in his thirties, and captivated by the new science of photography, Frith set out on a series of pioneering journeys up the Nile and to the Near East.

INTRIGUE AND EXPLORATION

He was the first photographer to venture beyond the sixth cataract of the Nile. Africa was still the mysterious 'Dark Continent', and Stanley and Livingstone's historic meeting was a decade into the future. The conditions for picture taking confound belief. He laboured for hours in his wicker dark-room in the sweltering heat of the desert, while the volatile chemicals fizzed dangerously in their trays. Back in London he exhibited his photographs and was 'rapturously cheered' by members of the Royal Society. His reputation as a photographer was made overnight.

VENTURE OF A LIFE-TIME

By the 1870s the railways had threaded their way across the country, and Bank Holidays and half-day Saturdays had been made obligatory by Act of Parliament. All of a sudden the working man and his family were able to enjoy days out, take holidays, and see a little more of the world.

With typical business acumen, Francis Frith foresaw that these new tourists would enjoy having souvenirs to commemorate their days out. For the next thirty years he travelled the country by train and by pony and trap, producing fine photographs of seaside resorts and beauty spots that were keenly bought by millions of Victorians. These prints were painstakingly pasted into family albums and pored over during the dark nights of winter, rekindling precious memories of summer excursions. Frith's studio was soon supplying retail shops all over the country, and by 1890 F Frith & Co had become the greatest specialist photographic publishing company in the world, with over 2,000 sales outlets, and pioneered the picture postcard.

FRANCIS FRITH'S LEGACY

Francis Frith had died in 1898 at his villa in Cannes, his great project still growing. By 1970 the archive he created contained over a third of a million pictures showing 7,000 British towns and villages.

Frith's legacy to us today is of immense significance and value, for the magnificent archive of evocative photographs he created provides a unique record of change in the cities, towns and villages throughout Britain over a century and more. Frith and his fellow studio photographers revisited locations many times down the years to update their views, compiling for us an enthralling and colourful pageant of British life and character.

We are fortunate that Frith was dedicated to recording the minutiae of everyday life. For it is this sheer wealth of visual data, the painstaking chronicle of changes in dress, transport, street layouts, buildings, housing and landscape that captivates us so much today, offering us a powerful link with the past and with the lives of our ancestors.

Computers have now made it possible for Frith's many thousands of images to be accessed almost instantly. The archive offers every one of us an opportunity to examine the places where we and our families have lived and worked down the years. Its images, depicting our shared past, are now bringing pleasure and enlightenment to millions around the world a century and more after his death.

For further information visit: www.francisfrith.com

INTERIOR DECORATION

Frith's photographs can be seen framed and as giant wall murals in thousands of pubs, restaurants, hotels, banks, retail stores and other public buildings throughout Britain. These provide interesting and attractive décor, generating strong local interest and acting as a powerful reminder of gentler days in our increasingly busy and frenetic world.

FRITH PRODUCTS

All Frith photographs are available as prints and posters in a variety of different sizes and styles. In the UK we also offer a range of other gift and stationery products illustrated with Frith photographs, although many of these are not available for delivery outside the UK – see our web site for more information on the products available for delivery in your country.

THE INTERNET

Over 100,000 photographs of Britain can be viewed and purchased on the Frith web site. The web site also includes memories and reminiscences contributed by our customers, who have personal knowledge of localities and of the people and properties depicted in Frith photographs. If you wish to learn more about a specific town or village you may find these reminiscences fascinating to browse. Why not add your own comments if you think they would be of interest to others? See **www.francisfrith.com**

PLEASE HELP US BRING FRITH'S PHOTOGRAPHS TO LIFE

Our authors do their best to recount the history of the places they write about. They give insights into how particular towns and villages developed, they describe the architecture of streets and buildings, and they discuss the lives of famous people who lived there. But however knowledgeable our authors are, the story they tell is necessarily incomplete.

Frith's photographs are so much more than plain historical documents. They are living proofs of the flow of human life down the generations. They show real people at real moments in history; and each of those people is the son or daughter of someone, the brother or sister, aunt or uncle, grandfather or grandmother of someone else. All of them lived, worked and played in the streets depicted in Frith's photographs.

We would be grateful if you would give us your insights into the places shown in our photographs: the streets and buildings, the shops, businesses and industries. Post your memories of life in those streets on the Frith website: what it was like growing up there, who ran the local shop and what shopping was like years ago; if your workplace is shown tell us about your working day and what the building is used for now. Read other visitors' memories and reconnect with your shared local history and heritage. With your help more and more Frith photographs can be brought to life, and vital memories preserved for posterity, and for the benefit of historians in the future.

Wherever possible, we will try to include some of your comments in future editions of our books. Moreover, if you spot errors in dates, titles or other facts, please let us know, because our archive records are not always completely accurate—they rely on 140 years of human endeavour and hand-compiled records. You can email us using the contact form on the website.

Thank you!

For further information, trade, or author enquiries
please contact us at the address below:

The Francis Frith Collection, Unit 6, Oakley Business Park, Wylye Road, Dinton, Wiltshire SP3 5EU England.
Tel: +44 (0)1722 716 376 Fax: +44 (0)1722 716 881
e-mail: sales@francisfrith.co.uk **www.francisfrith.com**